THE

DIVINE

DNA

ISAAC PITRE

RELIANT
PUBLISHING
A DIVISION OF REDEMPTION PRESS

Published by Reliant, an imprint of Redemption Press, PO Box 427, Enumclaw, WA 98022

Toll Free (844) 2REDEEM (273-3336)

Redemption Press is honored to present this title in partnership with the author. The views expressed or implied in this work are those of the author. Redemption Press provides our imprint seal representing design excellence, creative content, and high quality production.

Unless otherwise noted, all Scripture quotations are from The Holy Bible, King James Version.

Scripture quotations marked NKJV are from the Holy Bible, New King James Version. Copyright © 1982 by Thomas Nelson Publishers. Used by permission.

ISBN 13: 978-1-68314-995-8 (Paperback)
      978-1-68314-996-5 (ePub)
      978-1-68314-997-2 (Mobi)

Library of Congress Catalog Card Number: 2019912467

CONTENTS

Introduction

I am thrilled that you have chosen to read this book. It will give you an exciting new perspective on how God's "blueprint of life" has been implanted into both your physical and spiritual being. Even more, you will discover how, as a born-again believer, you have a genetic heritage that transforms you into the image of God.

As you will learn, the Creator has placed sacred strands of His being into you, waiting to be activated. His touch can transform your emotions, quicken your mind, and prepare you for a divine purpose.

You'll find the answers to these questions:

- How were we made, and why did God create us on this planet?
- Was the earth destroyed before the Garden of Eden?
- What is the important link between Satan's fall and Adam's fall?
- What is the separation between humanity and divinity?
- What part did Jesus play in restoring our Divine DNA?
- How are we affected by the three curses in the Garden?

- How can we win the battle between the flesh and the Spirit?
- What does God say concerning wealth and riches?
- What is our divine position, and why is it so significant?
- How can we live in the atmosphere of heaven?
- Why did Christ give us the keys to the Kingdom?
- How can we claim our royal heritage?
- Do we have the authority to rule and reign on earth?
- What is our role and responsibility in restoring God's kingdom?

As we address these questions, I want to show you how receiving Christ restores you to the person God intended you to be and gives you His life-changing characteristics.

It is your Divine DNA.

- Isaac Pitre

PART ONE

DIVINITY

CHAPTER ONE

THE "WHY" OF DIVINITY

What you are about to read is not speculation or supposition. It is based on God's truth and will give you answers to questions that have been raised through the ages:

- Why were we placed here on Planet Earth?
- What was God's intent and purpose for us?
- Exactly how was man made?

After reading the title of this book, perhaps you have a few additional questions: "What is Divine DNA?" "Is it something we automatically receive at birth?" "How can I know if it resides in me?"

The foundation of this truth comes from Psalm 8 when David declares:

> O LORD, our Lord, how excellent is thy name in all the earth! who hast set thy glory above the heavens. Out of the mouth of babes and sucklings hast thou ordained strength because of thine enemies, that thou mightest still the enemy and the avenger. When I consider thy heavens, the work of thy fingers, the moon and the stars, which thou hast ordained; What is man, that thou art mindful of him? and the son of man, that thou visitest him? For thou hast made him a little lower

than the angels, and hast crowned him with glory and honour. Thou madest him to have dominion over the works of thy hands; thou hast put all things under his feet. (Psalm 8:1-6)

The Divine DNA starts with, and encompasses, three different revelations and truths:

- Number one: God made man a little lower than the angels (verse 5). This is DIVINITY.
- Number two: God crowned man with glory and honor (verse 5). This is DIGNITY.
- Number three: God made man to rule over all the works of His hands and to put all things under His feet (verse 6). This is DOMINION.

SOLVING THE PUZZLE

So exactly what is divinity? It is that which is attributed to the Divine – who is God Almighty.

***

Since the beginning of time,
people have been searching for answers to understand
the meaning of their experience.

The psalmist was no different. His statement above reflects this eternal quest. After considering a God who, with the touch of His hand, created the moon, stars, and heavens, David asks, "What is man that You are mindful of him?" (Psalm 8:4 NKJV).

This was a thirst the psalmist was trying to quench.

To solve the puzzle, we have to return to the first chapter of Genesis where we find Moses writing about the Almighty's creation. In fact, I like to say that before you turn to Genesis 1, you have to go back to Genesis *zero* – which simply says: God!

Why? Because out of the Creator, all things began. Please understand that God did not begin. He has no beginning and no ending; He just *is*. Everything that exists came out of Him.

So, what we read in the first verse of the Bible is not the original beginning because the earth already existed by that time, and we are looking at its *destruction*.

You may ask, "How was that possible? Destruction before creation?"

Let's look at what Scripture tells us. It provides the answer to "What is Man?" and why God made us.

The Bible states, *"In the beginning God created the heaven and the earth"* (Genesis 1:1). The original world was made exactly like Him, perfect in splendor.

***

> **The earth was not formed as a wasteland,**
> **but was created just as glorious**
> **as heaven itself was made.**

It has always been God's desire that His will be done on earth as it is in heaven (Matthew 6:10). In other words, heaven and earth are to be in agreement with one another – both made in grandeur and glory.

The Fallen Angel

However, a cataclysmic event occurred in the beautiful world God had created – the world prior to the one written about in the second verse of the Bible, where we find, *"The earth was without form, and void"* (Genesis 1:2).

Yet before man, even before light, the Bible describes the fall of Lucifer into the realm of earth. We learn that God said he was the *"anointed cherub . . . and I have set thee so: thou wast upon the holy mountain of God; thou hast walked up and down in the midst of the stones of fire. Thou wast perfect in thy ways from the day that thou wast created, till iniquity was found in thee"* (Ezekiel 28:14-15).

Satan was made in the splendor and majesty of God. He was an angelic musician, the worship leader in heaven. The

Bible says of him: *"The workmanship of thy tabrets and of thy pipes was prepared in thee in the day that thou wast created"* (verse 13). When the wind of God blew through him, he presented melodies to the Almighty.

***

Satan's pride and ambition proved to be his undoing.

Scripture records: *"For thou hast said in thine heart, I will ascend into heaven, I will exalt my throne above the stars of God: I will sit also upon the mount of the congregation, in the sides of the north: I will ascend above the heights of the clouds; I will be like the most High"* (Isaiah 14:13-14).

It was because of this haughty, arrogant attitude that God declared, *"Yet thou shalt be brought down to hell, to the sides of the pit"* (verse 15).

Lucifer, the anointed angel, did not speak these words out loud. The Bible tells us Satan held these thoughts *"in thine heart"* – and the all-knowing God instantly banished him from heaven. So, to the devil's surprise, the next thought he entertained was on earth.

A BARREN WORLD

When Satan fell to earth, total confusion broke loose.

As is recorded in the first chapter of Genesis, after the downfall of Lucifer, this planet became a vast wasteland. Even more significant, *"darkness was upon the face of the deep"* (verse 2).

We know that the Almighty does not create darkness because Scripture tells us, *"God is light, and in him is no darkness at all"* (1 John 1:5). There is only one conclusion: God has no darkness to get darkness from!

The Hebrew words for *"without form and void"* let us know that the earth was a barren, purposeless place, a state of chaos with no order.

God didn't make it this way, yet this is the result of Satan's presence.

Redesigning the Earth

You may ask, "What does this have to do with our Divine DNA?"

This leads us back to discovering why God formed man.

The Creator looked down on the scene and made the decision to reorganize and restructure the earth to its original splendor and beauty.

Next, we find God separating light from darkness and night from day. He brings down the waters, which were above the firmament. Dry land appears, vegetation and fruit trees spring to life, and everything begins to reproduce after its own kind. There is harmony and order again. The birds are flying, the fish are swimming, the stars are shining, the moon is rising for the night shift, and the sun is ruling the day.

The world is blessed just as the Lord ordained it to be.

Then God, in all of His infinite wisdom, after He has rearranged His earth and returned it to its original grandeur, says to Himself, "How can I be sure that what I have created stays in harmony and agreement? How can I make certain it remains in order and retains the glorious splendor I intended – and manifests My brilliance and glory?"

From His vantage point in heaven, He sees Lucifer, a backslidden angel who has wreaked havoc in this realm. Yet God had now restructured everything to the way He first desired it to be.

***

The Creator questioned,
"How can I be assured this never happens again?"

The Answer to Chaos

God's answer for the turmoil, destruction, and disorder that plagued Planet Earth by the presence of Lucifer was this: *"Let us make man"* (Genesis 1:26).

Glory to God!

This meant man would be the answer to all of the upheaval the enemy brought to the earth realm. So man was placed here to govern so he could keep the order, beauty, splendor, and majesty which was now displayed.

The Bible records, *"And God said, Let us make man in our image, after our likeness: and let them have dominion over the fish of the sea, and over the fowl of the air, and over the cattle, and over all the earth, and over every creeping thing that creepeth upon the earth"* (Genesis 1:26).

Our heavenly Father not only made the decision to create man, but also to allow him to have "dominion" – to govern and be the steward of the earth.

Why was this control and oversight necessary? It was so the enemy (who now resided on earth) could no longer destroy what God had created.

This means that one of the reasons man was made was as a punishment for Lucifer's rebellion. We need to understand that when Satan fell from the heavens, he was delighted because he was no longer subjected to the governing power of the Almighty. Remember, he always wanted to be his own god, and his uprising is exactly what got him kicked out of heaven. The Lord said, "There is none like Me" – and cast him down.

In his new domain called earth, Satan began to set up his kingdom, his order, his throne. The result was total confusion and disorder. Yet the devil was in his element since he was totally in charge.

SATAN'S NEW MASTER

It is at this juncture God steps in to redesign what He has made. He is ready to create man and give him the power to govern the earth just as God would rule heaven.

So once more, Lucifer is about to be subservient – to again have an authority over him. This time it wouldn't be God; his new master would be man.

In essence, the Almighty was telling Satan, "I am going to lock you into a living arrangement with man, and he will have dominion over you. Not only did you once have to serve Me, but now you are required to serve him. You are going to be under man's authority and rule!"

***

Lucifer didn't escape dominion when he was barred from heaven. He soon learned that he had a new master in the form of man.

You can almost hear the devil wailing and screaming when he heard God say, "Let us make man in our image and after our likeness."

The concept of "image" deals with who man is and what he is – so that God would be made manifest in us. In addition, we were created in His "likeness" – dealing with how man is to function – again, like the heavenly Father, with authority and dominion.

This answers the question of why God made man. It was not only to reflect the image of the Creator, but to represent the Father here on earth.

"Represent" is a compound word. "Re" is a prefix, and "present" is what it is to do. So, to "re-present" God is what man was intended to accomplish. In the creation of Adam, we see God being presented again. The first man was the *re-presentation* of God.

Now that the "why" question has been dealt with, let's look at "how" God made man. It is here we begin to tap into the Divine DNA.

Chapter Two

The "How" of Divinity

The Bible describes how the Creator reached into the dust of the earth to make man. Please understand that the dust is not the man, but rather is the *form* the first human would be in.

Some uninformed people have tried to link the color of the dirt to the color of our skin – white dirt, brown dirt, yellow dirt, red dirt, or black dirt. Such thinking leads to racism and other divisions in society that cause dissension and bickering.

The dust which man was made from is simply ordinary dirt – and no person's dirt is superior to any other's. So as far as I am concerned, racism is the epitome of stupidity.

Since the earth is physical, God used a part of it to shape a physical body for man who would dwell on this planet.

Next, the Creator took what He had made and breathed into man's nostrils the breath of life. And, at that precise moment, man became a living soul.

Divinity in Humanity

What an amazing picture! There was just a clump of dirt lying on the ground, a corpse of clay, and God releases His spirit on the inside of this dirt and it miraculously comes alive. Man starts thinking, walking, and talking – all by the inspiration of what God breathed into him.

This leads to the inevitable conclusion that there is divinity in humanity:

- Humanity is the natural side of man – he has a body.
- Divinity is the spiritual side of man – he has the nature and life of God.

As we see this God-man walking around in the earth, it is "man-kind" which has been created.

God's Crowning Achievement

Consider the question of David once again. He asks, *"When I consider thy heavens, the work of thy fingers, the moon and the stars, which thou hast ordained; What is man, that thou art mindful of him?"* (Psalm 8:3-4).

Had the psalmist comprehended the true majesty of man, he would have understood that stars are nothing compared to what the Almighty formed from dust, and that man is the apex of God's creation.

***

We are the crowning achievement of all God is.

Everything we see, whether it is the sun, the moon, the stars, snowcapped mountain peaks, valleys, flowing streams, lilies, or roses that bloom – all of these wonders come out of the mind of God.

But when you see man, you are looking at a special creation, something that did not just spring from the mind of God – rather, the Almighty put His mind in man! And this is what separates us from the rest of creation.

We are the mind of God on this earth, taking charge of this planet just as He would.

Psalm 8:5 speaks of how we have been made *"a little lower than the angels."* In the Hebrew text, the word "angels" is written as *Elohim* – one of the names we use to characterize God.

So the scripture actually reads, "You made him a little lower than Yourself."

Again, we see the revelation of divinity, that man was made divine. Let me remind you, we are not God, but are made in the image and likeness of the Creator.

PARTAKERS OF THE DIVINE

When the Bible says that God breathed into Adam the breath of life, this means the Almighty released His Spirit or His nature on the inside of him – which means man was created to carry the nature of God.

We find additional truth concerning this in the New Testament. The apostle Peter writes, *"According as his divine power hath given unto us all things that pertain unto life and godliness, through the knowledge of him that hath called us to glory and virtue: whereby are given unto us exceeding great and precious promises: that by these ye might be partakers of the divine nature"* (2 Peter 1:3-4).

***

*It has always been God's will for man
to be part of divinity. In the mind and purpose of the
Father, it is the basic reason for our creation.*

Sadly, most people do not walk in their Divine DNA as they should because they do not see themselves as the Creator intended. "Divine" simply means that which is attributed to God – or God's attributes. As a result, we forfeit the divinity in us and live only in our humanity, bringing us to an existence which is lower than what God has called us to dwell in.

CATCHING THE BREATH OF GOD

Let's break down some of the characteristics of the divine nature of man.

As we have seen, the first man was made in the image of

God and had the Father's nature. Adam didn't need a Bible or a Sunday school lesson. He never attended a school of theology or a university. Instead, God's nature was simply downloaded into his inner man.

***

When the Lord breathes on you, more is caught than is taught!

I believe that when we begin to walk in communion with God as He designed for us to do, we will "catch," by a Divine DNA transfer, what can never be taught in a church service. And this is the will of God for us.

We know from Scripture that when the Lord and Adam had fellowship together, they were in a divine relationship.

TWO OF A KIND

Often, I hear people say that man was created to worship God. While this is true, an even higher reason for our creation was so we could walk in fellowship and communion with our Maker.

However, in order to have relationship, there must be two of a kind. The root word of "relationship" is *relate*. Thus, it is the practice of relating to one another – which requires that we be of the same kind. For example, I cannot have a true relationship with an ostrich or camel because there are too many differences.

This separation did not exist between God and Adam, because the first man was made in His image. We find them talking together *"in the cool of the day"* (Genesis 3:8).

The Hebrew for *"cool of the day"* is the same as "wind" or "breath" – what God breathed into Adam. This means the two of them talked spirit to spirit. They were in a dimension where they were able to relate to one another breath to breath, and this is how Adam was able to walk with God.

SATAN'S EVIL OBJECTIVE

Sadly, we know the tragic story of the fall of mankind, when Adam and Eve were deceived by God's archenemy, Lucifer, who appeared in the Garden of Eden in the guise of a serpent. He had only one objective: to cause man to fall from the state of being in the image and likeness of God. This, so the devil thought, would enable him to function in the earth realm once more without a Lord or Master over him.

His plan was to entice Adam to abdicate his throne by sinning against God.

***

*Satan knew firsthand that sin
would cause man to lose his position.*

His evil plan worked!

By succumbing to the devil's scheme, not only did Adam lose his authority in the earth, but he also lost his divine dimension.

Now, when the Lord came walking in the garden, He called out to Adam, *"Where art thou?"* (Genesis 3:9).

Of course, God knew exactly where Adam was. But because of the transgression, they were no longer talking spirit to spirit, breath to breath. Adam was not walking in the dimension God intended. This is why the Lord asked where he was.

THE SLIDE INTO MORAL DECAY

Adam still possessed a body and soul, but he had fallen from divinity to humanity. Yes, he continued to have a spirit, but no longer one that was divine. His mind, will, emotions, and intellect are still functioning; however, he has lost the DNA of God.

Thus, we see the birth of the Adamic nature. From this point forward, instead of being born with God's attributes, we find mankind now relegated to living beneath the divine nature of God.

Like Lucifer, man had slipped into a state of existing without God's DNA. This began the regression into decadence, depravity, and moral decay, generation after generation. As we read the Old Testament, we see how men and women had turned away from their Creator. No longer were they the true "sons of God."

"Sons" is the Greek word *genos,* which means those who carry the genes of a father. And so mankind no longer has the genes of God. They have lost the Divine DNA. As a result, murder, envy, rape, abuse, homosexuality, fear, anger, and bitterness are ruling society.

The Re-emergence of God's DNA

Let's fast forward forty-two generations. God had a plan to get His DNA back into man, and every time I think about this I want to shout Hallelujah!

The Bible declares that Jesus – the *genos* – with His Father's genes, came to the earth realm through a virgin for the purpose of allowing God's DNA to re-enter man.

Jesus not only was sent so that we could find a way of escape and enter heaven, but He also descended to earth to literally place the divinity of the Father back inside us. Why? So we could once more rule the earth like God rules the heavens, and we would again be in relationship with the Almighty – spirit to spirit – being true representatives of God in the earth.

The Great Exchange

I'm sure we all know the story of Calvary, but it is not my purpose here to present the theological and scriptural explanation of the death, burial, and resurrection. However, we need to understand that when Jesus rose from the grave, He conquered death.

When Christ died, He certainly did not cease to exist. It

was a state of being. The Bible declares that Jesus took sin upon Him, not habits or wrongdoings, but went to the cross with the very nature of sin – which was the Adamic nature.

What took place at Calvary was the great exchange.

***

Christ, who had the divine nature, removed it and placed upon Himself our carnal, Adamic nature, even though He had never sinned.

Jesus carried death to the cross, with all its wickedness, and was separated from God. The Father had to turn Himself away from His Son, because no one can stand before God with such a nature.

Scripture declares that Christ bore *"our sins in his own body on the tree, that we, being dead to sins, should live unto righteousness"* (1 Peter 2:24).

"THE GOD KIND OF LIFE"

God's Son did not sin, but He took on our transgressions at Calvary. He died a sinner's death, and therefore He gained access into a sinner's hell (Acts 2:31). But on the third day, God was satisfied that the price for sin's nature had been paid, and Jesus – right in the middle of hell – received again the Divine nature of God and was the first one born from death unto life.

By this, if we receive Him by faith, He gives us the right to now be called the sons of God.

This brings new meaning to this powerful statement: *"For God so loved the world, that he gave his only begotten Son, that whosoever believeth in him should not perish, but have everlasting life"* (John 3:16).

The term "everlasting life" in Greek is the word *zoe* – which means "the God kind of life." This is why Jesus came to earth and endured the agony of the cross.

The miracle that takes place in the born-again experience

is the same thing that happened to Jesus. We exchange our Adamic nature and spirit for the Divine DNA of God.

***

> *With the infusion of God breathing back into us His character and His personality, we begin once more to learn how to walk and live in the divine nature of God.*

Through the miracle of the new birth, we who had lost His DNA receive it back so we can begin again to live like God. What a glorious revelation and truth!

THE SUPERNATURAL SPHERE

Please don't come to the conclusion that being divine means you are going to be walking around on clouds or experiencing some mystical existence. No, God didn't make you as only a spirit, so He doesn't want you to be invisible like angels or move at the speed of light. Not at all. He made you divinity in human form because He wants you to operate in an earthly existence.

Let me explain it this way: God desires for you to be natural (your humanity), but not limited to only the natural, so He adds the "super," which is your divinity, so you can be "super-natural."

As a result, we are able to function in the natural and physical spheres, yet are not bound by these. We are also in a realm that is spiritual so we can hear from God and see as He sees – becoming a supernatural being.

MANIFESTATIONS OF LOVE

To comprehend your Divine DNA, you have to understand the inherent qualities in your heavenly Father.

The Bible provides the answer when it tells us: *"But the*

fruit of the Spirit is love, joy, peace, longsuffering, gentleness, goodness, faith, meekness, temperance: against such there is no law" (Galatians 5:22-23).

These are not different selections of fruit; rather, they are one – with several slices, just like an orange.

Those listed above are all manifestations of one fruit – love. The nature and DNA of God is love, yet it seems to be the one thing Christians have the most difficulty with. Why? Because learning to love is more than natural or emotional. Sure, there are feelings involved, but real love is spiritual.

NOT AN "IT"

When you study the Scriptures, you discover that love is not an "it" – love is a "Who." The Bible clearly tells us that *"God is love"* (1 John 4:8), and He who is love imparted His DNA into us.

***

Through salvation, what is of God becomes ours,
so love is now part of our nature.

Scripture explains, *"Love suffers longs and is kind; love does not envy; love does not parade itself, is not puffed up; does not behave rudely, does not seek its own, is not provoked, thinks no evil; does not rejoice in iniquity, but rejoices in the truth; bears all things, believes all things, hopes all things, endures all things"* (1 Corinthians 13:4-7 NKJV).

This is a mirror of what we read in Galatians 5, and it reinforces the fact that love is the divine nature of our heavenly Father:

- God heals because He loves.
- God delivers because He loves.
- God guides because He loves.

***

> *It's because of His unending love that the Lord instructs,*
> *rebukes, encourages, and even chastises us.*

Oh, for the day God's children begin to walk in the nature of His love and realize it is more than a candlelit dinner or a bouquet of roses.

A NEW PERSPECTIVE

When the Lord's true nature becomes ours, we will begin to have the perspective of the Almighty. Jesus proclaimed: *"A new commandment I give unto you, That ye love one another; as I have loved you, that ye also love one another"* (John 13:34). And He added, *"By this shall all men know that ye are my disciples, if ye have love one to another"* (verse 35).

This is not a popular message because we are living in a day when, as the Bible declares, *"the love of many shall wax cold"* (Matthew 24:12).

In our natural, carnal state, we are reluctant to love, encourage, be patient, gentle, longsuffering, or exhibit self-control. Yet the greatest call to a believer is to walk in the image of God and represent His divine nature on earth.

Are you hearing His voice?

Chapter Three

The "Who" of Divinity

In the first two chapters we have zeroed in on the "Why" and "How" of divinity, but our Divine DNA would never be possible without a "Who."

It is only because of the divine nature of God that we can possess the attributes and qualities of the Creator. Through Christ we have a bloodline to the Father that proves we are children of the King.

There's an old saying that goes, "The proof is in the pudding," and we can prove we have royal blood flowing through our veins by how we have been miraculously transformed. As Scripture says, *"Therefore if any man be in Christ, he is a new creature: old things are passed away; behold, all things are become new"* (2 Corinthians 5:17).

Our old DNA is no longer relevant because it has been replaced by the blood of Christ. We are not just transformed by what we think or say, but rather we are new creatures – which means every part of us has been divinely changed.

Escaping the Past

The fact that we have undergone a spiritual "blood trans-fusion" makes us legal heirs to everything in God's kingdom. *"The Spirit itself beareth witness with our spirit, that we are the children of God: And if children, then heirs; heirs of God, and joint-heirs with Christ"* (Romans 8:16-17).

The struggle most believers have is the constant tug-of-war between their humanity and their divinity. The problems exist because the past is so difficult to escape.

Before we were born again, our former nature controlled us. So:

- Our minds thought
- Our wills decided
- Our emotions felt
- Our imaginations visualized
- Our bodies craved

What were we thinking, deciding, feeling, visualizing, and craving? Those things which were carnal and had been planted in us by the brainwashing of Lucifer.

***

We are no different than Adam.
When he lost God's nature,
he had no other source to draw on except the enemy.

So, when the first man disconnected from the Creator, he plugged right into Satan – and we know the tragic results.

Adam's decision still affects you and me. Yes, we have been born again and now have Divine DNA as part of our new nature, but our minds have spent years and years being exposed to wickedness. This is why the apostle Paul tells us, *"And be not conformed to this world: but be ye transformed by the renewing of your mind, that ye may prove what is that good, and acceptable, and perfect, will of God"* (Romans 12:2).

TIME FOR RETRAINING

What is your part in this process of change?

- You have to retrain your mind to think
- You have to retrain your emotions to feel
- You have to retrain your will to act or to decide
- You have to retrain your body with new appetites and desires

***

***You can no longer behave as you did when
you were controlled by your Adamic nature.***

The Bible advises us: *"Walk in the Spirit, and ye shall not
fulfil the lust of the flesh. For the flesh lusteth against the Spirit,
and the Spirit against the flesh: and these are contrary the one to
the other: so that ye cannot do the things that ye would"* (Galatians
5:16-17).

Read these verses often. They are powerful!

GOOD VS. EVIL

There's a fierce battle raging. Our Divine DNA is warring
against the residue of our old nature. Our prior thoughts, arrogance, fear, pride – and an endless list of negative behaviors –
are in mortal combat with the new divinity within us.

Paul confessed this when he wrote:

> For we know that the law is spiritual: but I am carnal,
> sold under sin. For that which I do I allow not: for what
> I would, that do I not; but what I hate, that do I.
>
> If then I do that which I would not, I consent unto
> the law that it is good. Now then it is no more I that
> do it, but sin that dwelleth in me. For I know that in
> me (that is, in my flesh,) dwelleth no good thing: for to
> will is present with me; but how to perform that which

is good I find not.

For the good that I would I do not: but the evil which I would not, that I do. Now if I do that I would not, it is no more I that do it, but sin that dwelleth in me. I find then a law, that, when I would do good, evil is present with me.

For I delight in the law of God after the inward man: But I see another law in my members, warring against the law of my mind, and bringing me into captivity to the law of sin which is in my members.

O wretched man that I am! who shall deliver me from the body of this death? I thank God through Jesus Christ our Lord. (Romans 7:14-25)

Yet after all this soul searching, Paul was able to declare, *"There is therefore now no condemnation to them which are in Christ Jesus, who walk not after the flesh, but after the Spirit"* (Romans 8:1).

WORKS OF THE FLESH

The Bible has much to say concerning spiritual warfare, but it is more about the Adamic than the demonic. In fact, Satan needs original sin in order to function. The battle we personally face is between the residue of what remains on our souls and bodies that wrestles against our new, divine self.

***

The "works of the flesh" continue to plague us because after Adam lost God's nature he fell under the power of Lucifer, who used him in order to carry out his satanic desires on earth.

This connection continues in man to this very day, and only through the new birth do we have a chance to break free.

Scripture warns us, *"The works of the flesh are manifest, which are these; adultery, fornication, uncleanness, lasciviousness, idolatry, witchcraft, hatred, variance, emulations, wrath, strife, seditions, heresies, envyings, murders, drunkenness, revellings, and such like: of the which I tell you before, as I have also told you in time past, that they which do such things shall not inherit the kingdom of God"* (Galatians 5:19-21).

All of these fleshly tendencies reside in the nature we were born with. I am not saying that every man or woman who has not experienced the new birth will commit adultery, but the inclination is unbridled without the God-consciousness which comes with our salvation.

ETERNAL LIFE NOW

The reason Jesus said to Nicodemus, "Ye must be born again" (John 3:7), is because He saw the beginning from the end. Jesus knew that if our character remains in the state of the Adamic, influenced by the demonic, it is only a matter of time before sin becomes manifest and lives are destroyed.

***

Even though heaven is our eternal home and our blessed hope, there are enormous benefits to the born-again experience for the here and now.

Let me express it another way: Eternal life is not what you receive when you get to heaven; you must have eternal life to *go* there. It is a prerequisite for walking through the pearly gates.

An individual without God's nature is not allowed access to the eternal city. While being born again gives us admission to heaven, it is also necessary so we do not make a wreck of our lives while here on earth.

BORN IN SIN

Satan's goal is to *"steal, and to kill, and to destroy"* (John 10:10). He plots and schemes to have us bound and stymied by depression, fear, low self-esteem, hatred, lust, and perversion.

It was never God's will for you and me to live like this, but because of the original transgression in the Garden of Eden, we were all born in sin and *"shapen in iniquity"* (Psalm 51:5).

I have the most beautiful daughter any father could ask for. But inside of all her beauty, because of Adam, she was created with a sinful nature:

- I didn't have to teach her how to lie.
- I didn't have to teach her disobedience.
- I didn't have to teach her pride.
- I didn't have to teach her arrogance.

All of these things are active and present in every person at birth because each of us entered this world outside the divine nature of God.

***

> ***Only redemption through Christ can erase the sin we were born with and give us new Divine DNA.***

GOD'S DISAPPOINTMENT

After man lost the divinity and the image of God, his nature went haywire. I can see the disappointment on the countenance of the Creator as He looks down and sees man acting much like animals, carrying out the evil plans of Lucifer.

The Bible records: *"God saw that the wickedness of man was great in the earth, and that every imagination of the thoughts of his heart was only evil continually. And it repented the Lord that he had made man on the earth, and it grieved him at his heart"* (Genesis 6:5-6).

This is why God sent the flood – because humanity was no longer carrying out the reason for which it was created. Why was man placed here? To fulfill the purpose of the Almighty.

A NEW RESPONSE

The answer to the works of the flesh is to welcome and embrace the fruit of the Spirit, which we discussed earlier (Galatians 5:22-23).

This is inherently, intrinsically implanted into the heart, mind, and soul of a person who is born again – who has received the divine nature of God He always intended for us to have. The "fruit" becomes your *new* self.

Since love is now alive within us, our actions are different today than they were yesterday. For example, when I hear that two believers are bickering and unable to get along, it tells me that one of them is not walking in their divinity.

Dissension is part of the "old man" – the flesh.

I am convinced that the reason we struggle in Christianity with divorce, church splits, and even racial divisions, is because believers are not operating in the divinity available to them.

When you truly understand that you have been made in the likeness of God, it will be natural to love the unlovable and forgive the unforgivable.

- How will you respond when people mistreat you?
- What will you say when they gossip or lie about you?
- What if you are taken advantage of in a business transaction?

Your former self will tell you to lash out and retaliate any way you can. But now you're a new creation, with love at the core of your spirit, so your response is different.

This is not to say you will be passive or willing to be mistreated. This is far from the truth.

A CALM ANSWER

There are individuals who rationalize and say they stay in

an abusive situation because of love. That's not love – because it is not God's character to either abuse or to be abused.

***

Did Jesus allow people to misuse Him? Not at all.

When the Lord's harshest critics gathered around Him with their angry questions, He didn't respond with wrath, but with a calm, loving spirit.

One morning while Jesus was teaching in the temple, the scribes and Pharisees brought a woman to Him who was accused of adultery. As Scripture records:

> They say unto him, Master, this woman was taken in adultery, in the very act. Now Moses in the law commanded us, that such should be stoned: but what sayest thou?
>
> This they said, tempting him, that they might have to accuse him. But Jesus stooped down, and with his finger wrote on the ground, as though he heard them not.
>
> So when they continued asking him, he lifted up himself, and said unto them, He that is without sin among you, let him first cast a stone at her. And again he stooped down, and wrote on the ground.
>
> And they which heard it, being convicted by their own conscience, went out one by one, beginning at the eldest, even unto the last: and Jesus was left alone, and the woman standing in the midst. (John 8:4-9)

JOY AND PEACE

Other attributes of our "new man" produce the same positive results. For example, it is now my nature to be joyful. Therefore, joy is not a feeling; it is a spiritual force – part of the Divine DNA of God.

This is also true regarding peace. To walk in true peace is not dependent on what happens to you; it is a work of the Spirit that is planted within you. As a result, by walking in this truth you should never be rattled by the situations raging around you.

***

Your life will be guarded from turmoil, trauma, and stress.

The Word promises, *"And the peace of God, which passeth all understanding, shall keep your hearts and minds through Christ Jesus"* (Philippians 4:7).

"I'M NOT GOING TO PANIC!"

With your new nature, when trouble hits head-on you can stand to your feet, throw your shoulders back, and confidently say, "I'm not going to panic!" You don't even need to attempt to fix the situation in your own strength.

This is possible because of what has taken place in your heart and soul. Of course, the battle we discussed earlier will continue to be fought. Your old carnal man will whisper in your ear, "You'd better be worried! You will never get out of this mess!"

The enemy's goal is to cause your emotions to react just as they did during the years you were influenced and trained by what is demonic. So, you confront Satan and say, "No! I have the peace of God!"

The new you is also longsuffering, because love doesn't keep a record of wrongdoing (1 Corinthians 13:5).

***

Because of this amazing change, forgiveness, kindness, gentleness, and self-control are now part of your lifestyle.

These qualities have been grafted into your Divine DNA so you can live like the Christian God intended you to be.

THE COMFORTER

Just before Jesus left the earth and ascended back to heaven to sit at the right hand of the Father, He gave this promise: *"And I will pray the Father, and he shall give you another Comforter, that he may abide with you for ever; even the Spirit of truth; whom the world cannot receive, because it seeth him not, neither knoweth him; but ye know him; for he dwelleth with you, and shall be in you. I will not leave you comfortless"* (John 14:16-18).

And He added, *"But the Comforter, which is the Holy Ghost, whom the Father will send in my name, he shall teach you all things, and bring all things to your remembrance, whatsoever I have said unto you."* (verse 26).

The Holy Spirit *did* appear and is here on earth at this very moment and is walking alongside you as your Counselor, Teacher, and Guide.

He is also *"in you,"* bringing things *"to your remembrance,"* providing you with wisdom and understanding. Even more, we have been given the Spirit's *"power from on high"* (Luke 24:49).

This is why we can live with strength and courage and can face any challenge. Remember, *"God hath not given us the spirit of fear; but of power, and of love, and of a sound mind"* (2 Timothy 1:7). This means it is not in our DNA to be fearful or timid, but rather to be strong in the Lord and courageous, because *"the righteous are bold as a lion"* (Proverbs 28:1). We must never forget that our heavenly Father is the Lion of the tribe of Judah (Revelation 5:5).

Glory to God!

LED BY THE SPIRIT

The prophet Isaiah presents the characteristics of the coming Messiah when he writes, *"And the spirit of the Lord shall rest upon him, the spirit of wisdom and understanding, the spirit of counsel and might, the spirit of knowledge and of the fear of the Lord"* (Isaiah 11:2).

Because we have accepted God's Son by faith and our hearts have been cleansed by His blood, these things are now in our very being – which gives us the divine ability to flow and function in the supernatural gifts of the Spirit.

Since one of the gifts manifested in you is knowledge, the ability to know, don't ignore what it means to be "led by the Spirit." Sometimes it may come as a hunch, an intuition, or a check in your spirit that gives a warning. It is part of our divine nature we should listen to and obey.

You Reflect Who He Is

You and I were made in God's image and likeness and are His sons and daughters. You were produced out of His genes, yet the son is never greater than the Father. So to Him be majesty, honor, dominion, and power. Even more, as a believer, you are a partaker of His divine nature and reflect who He is.

Be thankful every day that you have personally met the "Who" of divinity – God the Father, God the Son, and God the Holy Spirit.

PART TWO

DIGNITY

Chapter Four

You Are Crowned
with Glory

From the moment of our salvation, we should rejoice every day that we have been given the divinity of God Himself. At the same time, we received a second major blessing from the Almighty. Although we did not ask for it, the Lord gave us *dignity*.

In order to better understand this revelation, let's look again at the words of the psalmist: *"What is man, that thou are mindful of him? and the son of man, that thou visitest him? For thou hast made him a little lower than the angels, and hast crowned him with glory and honour"* (Psalm 8:4-5).

How amazing! A brilliant crown denoting glory and honor has been placed on your head.

A Paradise of Riches

To fully grasp the significance of the gift, we have to take a closer look at what happened at the beginning of time. After God formed man from the dust of the ground and breathed into his nostrils, he became a living being. Next we find Adam being ushered into a place of glory and honor.

As Scripture chronicles:

The Lord God planted a garden eastward in Eden, and

> there He put the man whom He had formed. And out
> of the ground the Lord God made every tree grow that
> is pleasant to the sight and good for food. The tree of
> life was also in the midst of the garden, and the tree of
> the knowledge of good and evil.
>
> Now a river went out of Eden to water the garden,
> and from there it parted and became four riverheads.
> The name of first is Pishon; it is the one which skirts
> the whole land of Havilah, where there is gold. And the
> gold of that land is good. Bdellium and the onyx stone
> are there. (Genesis 2:8-12 NKJV)

God not only gave Adam and Eve a perfect garden in which
to live, but He also blessed them with unbelievable riches –
land filled with gold and precious stones.

This tells us that man was not made to acquire wealth, but
to be wealth! It was his from the start.

***

Friend, this is part of your Divine DNA.
The abundance of the world was given
to you in the beginning.

A GLORIOUS BURDEN

It's exciting to know what it means to be crowned with
glory and honor.

"Glory" is the Hebrew word *kabode,* which is translated as
to have something on you that is heavy. So when God's Word
tells us that glory has been placed on our lives, it is weighty and
filled with abundance.

The same word in biblical Greek is *doxa*, which denotes the
true comprehension of a thing – its intrinsic value.

***

Man was made to manifest the glory of God.

It is immaterial whether you were born on the wrong side of the tracks or in a place with no tracks at all! Part of your Divine DNA in your reborn spirit is exactly what God originally purposed in Adam. His nature carried the essence of the Creator.

Today the Lord wants this same glory to be yours. As the apostle Paul writes, *"But we all, with open face beholding as in a glass the glory of the Lord, are changed into the same image from glory to glory, even as by the Spirit of the Lord"* (2 Corinthians 3:18).

What a glorious transformation!

The Source of Honor

In the Garden of Eden, man was also crowned with honor.

In the original language, "honor" is translated as magnificent – an ornament, a splendor of beauty and excellence. Man was the majesty of God.

You were made to be superior and more impressive than anything the Almighty created – including the stars and the mountains.

Honor, however, is a gift of God, and only when He bestows it upon you does it have true meaning.

When Solomon was about to become king of Israel, God asked him what he wished for. To everyone's surprise, he didn't request wealth or prestige, but wisdom and a heart to understand the people. As a result of his humility, the Lord gave him what he asked for – and so much more.

God told Solomon, *"Behold, I have done according to thy words: lo, I have given thee a wise and an understanding heart; so that there was none like thee before thee, neither after thee shall any arise like unto thee. And I have also given thee that which thou hast not asked, both riches, and honour: so that there shall not be any among the kings like unto thee all thy days"* (1 Kings 3:12-13).

It wasn't Solomon who gave himself honor – it was a gift from the Almighty.

GOD'S SPLENDOR IS YOURS

It is the glory and honor granted by the Lord that allows you to have the dignity to truly represent Him.

When some people hear the word "dignified," they often bring to mind an individual who is filled with their own importance, but this is a misuse of the word. Dignity simply means that which God has bestowed great honor upon, just as an earthly dignitary is a person of high esteem.

***

When we are born again and children of the Most High God, we have an obligation to carry ourselves in a dignified manner, one which represents His excellence and splendor.

When Scripture speaks of man being "crowned," it refers to the will of the Creator to have us encompassed and surrounded by an environment of heaven itself. Everywhere Adam turned, he saw the essence of God – His grandeur, beauty, wealth, and majesty.

This perfect setting was conducive for man's growth and development.

Today, as a born-again believer, you have been ushered into God's kingdom. And He longs to place the same crown of glory and honor on you.

Are you ready to walk worthy of His calling?

When you were born-again something amazing and supernatural happened. You were officially coronated by God. Although you were not aware of it, a ceremony occurred, and in this ceremony, you were crowned by God. It is important for you to understand that you did not just receive glory and honor, but God placed His glory and honor on you. The word *honor* in Greek is the word "time". It means value, or highest degree of esteem. So, when you were born-again and received back His image, God declared His worth over you – which means you carry the value of the Almighty on your life. Let that sink into your mind for a second, the fact that God says, "I esteem you to the highest degree because you are My child." And because God has declared your worth, this means you should never struggle with low self-esteem.

When you were born-again your status changed. You went from a sinner to a king. All of God's kids are kings. This is why you carry so much honor and weight. The Bible declares in that we have been adopted by our heavenly Father: "*And if children, then heirs; heirs of God, and joint-heirs with Christ*" (Romans 8:17). Glory to God! That means I am royalty.

Receive Your Inheritance

Picture this with me for a moment. When you were saved you stood before the throne of God and the Father looked at you and said, "You are no longer an orphan or a sinner, you are My heir." So, with all the angels watching, God took His hands and laid them on you and declared, "Be blessed my child and receive your inheritance. I bestow upon you My glory, My honor, and My name."

Wow! That's the concept you need to cherish regarding what happened when you were born into the family of God.

Now that we realize that we have been crowned or adorned with this high level of majesty and honor, we can better understand how God "*raised us up together, and made us sit together in the heavenly places in Christ Jesus*" (Ephesians 2:6 NKJV).

You hold an exalted position with God. You are no longer just a sinner saved by grace. You *were* a sinner and now His grace has made you son. Therefore, live in the value that God has placed on you. See yourself as He does. Jesus died to give you back this position, so don't abdicate your inheritance. You are a representative of the family of God, so act like it.

Now that God Himself has told me what I'm worth and just how highly He values me, it lets me know what I deserve. The very best! When God place His honor on my life, He was telling me that I am worth everything to Him. Remember, it was His glory and honor which was bestowed. This means I don't walk around in *my* worth, I walk around in *His* worth. Glory to God!

I know it's hared to believe, but you carry on you heaven's price tag. You are more valuable than you realize. The reason this is so vital is because Proverbs 23: 7 says, "*As a man thinketh in his hear, so is he.*" We are not living the life of a king, because we don't see ourselves as kings.

Today, God wants you to stop settling for less and walk in the glory and honor He has given you.

CHAPTER FIVE

START LIVING IN THE ATMOSPHERE OF HEAVEN

Heaven is breathtaking!

There are people who have died and declared they have gone to heaven, yet found it difficult to describe what they saw. Baptist minister Don Piper, for example, was pronounced dead at the scene of an automobile accident. Yet an hour and a half later, while being prayed for by a fellow pastor, he suddenly came back to life. Piper is the author of *90 Minutes in Heaven*, a bestselling book in which he tells what it was like to be in heaven, if only for a short time.

In Piper's words, "I looked around and the sight overwhelmed me. Coming out from the gate – a short distance ahead – was a brilliance that was brighter than the light that surrounded us, utterly luminous. In trying to describe the scene, words are totally inadequate, because human words can't express the feeling of awe and wonder at what I beheld."

BEYOND IMAGINATION

This reflects what the Bible states regarding what lies ahead: *"Eye hath not seen, nor ear heard, neither have entered into the heart of man, the things which God hath prepared for them that love him"* (1 Corinthians 2:9). And even those who have been allowed to see the celestial city through a vision are rendered almost speechless.

However, God did give us a glimpse of His abode by what He created on earth for the first man.

You see, it was always the purpose of our heavenly Father that His *"will be done in earth, as it is in heaven"* (Matthew 6:10).

So, if God was going to put Himself in man, then Adam – who was in the image of the Creator – would need the same kind of environment God enjoyed in order to function.

This is why He designed the Garden of Eden before He made man.

***

The Lord needed to provide the surroundings
that resembled heaven itself.

THE AMBIANCE OF THE ALMIGHTY

It was God's decision to make a place of beauty, glory, excellence, and wealth.

Essentially, the Creator was saying, "If I am going to dwell in man on the earth, he must be in the same atmosphere that resembles My own home."

So, God formed a paradise in preparation for Adam and Eve because He knew that if man had the nature of God, he would need to live in the ambiance of the Almighty.

Pardon my bluntness, but I want to challenge those in the body of Christ who feel it is not God's will for us to prosper and have the very best. On the contrary, it is the only environment in which your nature is completely at peace.

THE ESSENCE OF WHO YOU ARE

Perhaps you are struggling at this present moment – worried to the point of desperation over your rent or mortgage payments. Maybe you are driving a car that is on its last wheels, about to break down, or are you raising five active kids in a two-bedroom apartment. It could be you are depressed over your job, one you are thankful for, but really don't enjoy – however, you have no other choice since the bills have to be paid and food has to be put on the table.

All of these factors may be choking your Divine DNA, stifling the essence of who you are, and suffocating your creativity.

This is happening because your spirit was made to function in an atmosphere of glory and honor. It was built to operate in an arena of wealth, prosperity, and dignity – a place of total comfort.

We are not speaking of man's desire, but of God's will for him. In Eden, everything was *"pleasant to the sight"* (Genesis 2:9) – which means wherever Adam looked, it was absolutely beautiful.

DOES EXCELLENCE ENVELOP YOUR EXISTENCE?

What about today? Do you think God wants for you to be surrounded by anything less than His splendor? Of course not.

***

There's nothing wrong in desiring a better home or a piece of property with a picturesque view.

This expectation is inherently in you because God "wired us" to be in a place that wherever we look, we love what we see! This is why it is important for you to pursue the house of your dreams – a dwelling in which, when you wake up each morning, your spirit feels at home.

Some of the frustration you may be feeling right now is because wherever you look, nothing relates to your nature. For some this may mean a washing machine that's on the blink, furniture that desperately needs to be reupholstered, or wallpaper that is peeling off the walls.

As a result, there is no peace and tranquility, no excellence surrounding your existence.

BRING OUT THE BEST

The right environment is absolutely essential – not only for beauty, but also for growth and development.

- A plant must be placed in the right soil in order to bloom.
- A fish must stay in the water in order to survive.
- A star must remain in the sky in order to shine.

Since this is true, man must be in an atmosphere of glory in order for his best to be released.

TOTAL PROVISION

It is significant that in the Garden of Eden, every tree was not only beautiful to look at, but was also *"good for food"* (Genesis 3:6).

Adam was in a sanctuary of total provision, which means mankind was made to function in an environment where every need was met. Even more, the Bible says the Creator made the trees to grow (Genesis 2:9). This tells us that it was God's will to have a place for man where He supplied everything needed for living.

Of course, Adam would have to cultivate and tend the garden, but he was not responsible for its abundance. God said, *"I have given you every herb bearing seed, which is upon the face of all the earth, and every tree, in the which is the fruit of a tree yielding seed; to you it shall be for meat"* (Genesis 1:29).

From the moment Adam first opened his eyes, everywhere he looked there was plump, ripe fruit growing for him to pick and enjoy.

It was the Father's great delight to supply every necessity.

Why? Because He is a God of provision.

PLANNED IN HEAVEN

Much has been said concerning the prosperity message and those who preach it, but when you study Scripture, you discover that from the beginning, God was determined to meet every necessity. So we need to stop apologizing for the goodness of God. It is part of His original blueprint and design.

Adam did not ask for this land of abundance; it was God's decision. He simply entered a world of grandeur that was planned in heaven.

***

The first man discovered what it meant to be in God's glory, with everything at his disposal.

This is why I emphasize that if you are struggling for provision and are stressed to the point your blood pressure is rising and your physical health is in jeopardy, there is no reason.

It goes back to the original conflict. We were created to have all things provided for. Our nature doesn't know how to respond in stress and strain because it is grafted in our DNA to live in prosperity.

But to truly get the picture of this divine provision, we also have to understand how it was taken away by the fall of man.

SATAN'S LIE

Of the countless trees growing in the Garden of Eden that provided food, there was only one that was off limits. Regarding this particular tree, God said, "Do not touch it!"

Specifically, the Creator told Adam, *"Of every tree of the garden you may freely eat; but of the tree of the knowledge of good and evil you shall not eat, for in the day that you eat of it you shall surely die"* (Genesis 2:16-17 NKJV).

Satan was well aware of this, so he devised a scheme that resulted in the original sin. The Bible records:

> Now the serpent was more cunning than any beast of the field which the Lord God had made. And he said to the woman, "Has God indeed said, 'You shall not eat of every tree of the garden'?"
>
> And the woman said to the serpent, "We may eat the fruit of the trees of the garden; but of the fruit of the tree which is in the midst of the garden, God has said, 'You shall not eat it, nor shall you touch it, lest you die.'"
>
> Then the serpent said to the woman, "You will not surely die. For God knows that in the day you eat of it your eyes will be opened, and you will be like God, knowing good and evil." So when the woman saw that the tree was good for food, that it was pleasant to the eyes, and a tree desirable to make one wise, she took of its fruit and ate. She also gave to her husband with her, and he ate.
>
> Then the eyes of both of them were opened, and they knew that they were naked; and they sewed fig leaves together and made themselves coverings. And they heard the sound of the Lord God walking in the garden in the cool of the day, and Adam and his wife hid themselves from the presence of the Lord God among the trees of the garden.
> Then the Lord God called to Adam and said to him, "Where are you?"
>
> So he said, "I heard Your voice in the garden, and I was afraid because I was naked; and I hid myself."
>
> And He said, "Who told you that you were naked? Have you eaten from the tree of which I commanded you that you should not eat?"
>
> Then the man said, "The woman whom You gave to be with me, she gave me of the tree, and I ate."
> And the Lord God said to the woman, "What is this you have done?" The woman said, "The serpent deceived me, and I ate." (Genesis 3:1-13 NKJV)

The Three Curses

The devil tempted Adam and Eve with the same desire that caused his own downfall. He told them if they ate of this tree of knowledge, *"You will be like God"* (verse 5).

The truth was, they were already like God, made in His image and likeness. But because of their disobedience, the Almighty had no other choice but to declare punishment for sin – with three separate curses.

The first curse was on Satan. God told him, *"Because you have done this, you are cursed more than all cattle, and more than every beast of the field; on your belly you shall go, and you shall eat dust all the days of your life. And I will put enmity between you and the woman, and between your seed and her Seed; He shall bruise your head, and you shall bruise His heel"* (Genesis 3:14-15 NKJV).

The second curse was placed on the woman: *"I will greatly multiply your sorrow and your conception; in pain you shall bring forth children; your desire shall be for your husband, and he shall rule over you"* (verse 16 NKJV).

God's final curse was on man: *"Cursed is the ground for your sake; in toil you shall eat of it all the days of your life. Both thorns and thistles it shall bring forth for you, and you shall eat the herb of the field. In the sweat of your face you shall eat bread till you return to the ground, for out of it you were taken; for dust you are, and to dust you shall return"* (verses 17-19 NKJV).

Goodbye, Paradise!

What a turnaround! Remember, it was God's will for man to live in a place of total provision and prosperity. But because of Adam's sin, the Almighty announced, "I am no longer going to supply your every need. You will have to work by the sweat of your brow to succeed."

***

Adam was forced to give up the lifestyle of the garden paradise with its atmosphere of beauty, honor, supply, and dignity.

Now he would have to physically break up the hard, arid soil, water his crops, and toil for survival.

This was quite a dramatic departure from God's original plan, but even though he tried to use Eve as an excuse, Adam had no one to blame but himself.

REDUCED TO A LIFE OF TRAVAIL

The curse brought hard labor – which exists to this very day. I've heard many complain, "Why is life so difficult?"

For millions, the answer lies in the fact that they have not repented of their sin and made a decision to live in the presence of God.

The Bible tells us, *"the way of transgressors is hard"* (Proverbs 13:15). Life becomes tedious. This is why men begin to steal and even kill. We see this evidenced in the life of the sons of Adam and Eve. Abel tended sheep, while Cain tilled the soil. Both brought an offering to the Lord: Cain offered some of his fruit, but Abel presented *"the firstlings of his flock and of the fat thereof"* (Genesis 4:4).

When God responded with special honor to Abel's offering, Cain became so jealous and outraged that he killed his brother in the field (verse 8).

Because of iniquity, man was driven from honor. He was no longer the dignity of God, but was reduced to a life of labor and travail.

This is the world we were all born into, but those who have accepted Christ and have been infused with God's Divine DNA are now delivered from the curse of the ground, from the thorns and thistles.

Yes, we are required to work, but it becomes a joy rather than a burden, a labor of love instead of a heavy task, because we know the eternal reward that awaits us.

We have now been repositioned as sons and daughters of the Living God. The curse that was pronounced on Adam is lifted, and we are invited to enjoy a life of Garden living again! Praise the Lord!

We have been graciously restored to the place we lost.

Your Divine Position

Let me share an exciting truth with you. It involves positions and conditions.

When you understand that wealth is your position, then you will have faith to change your condition.

You may be reading this book in one of the poorest economically deprived nations on earth – such as Sudan, Haiti, or Cambodia. Be encouraged today. It makes no difference where or how you live; if you realize your position of favor with God, He will begin to move in your circumstances and give you the lifestyle and atmosphere He ordained for you.

According to Scripture, "The blessing of the Lord, it maketh rich, and he addeth no sorrow with it" (Proverbs 10:22).

This is the favor God gave mankind in Genesis 1, and it is His will that we operate in this divine provision.

***

Since wealth is your position, it is automatically your condition – which means it is the Father's intent to manifest in your life the things that contribute to your place in His kingdom.

The Covenant

The wealth provided by heaven brings not only dignity, but also brings power and authority as sons of God. The Bible says,

"You shall remember the Lord your God, for it is He who gives you power to get wealth, that He may establish His covenant which He swore to your fathers" (Deuteronomy 8:18 NKJV).

Someone once said to me, "I thought the covenant God made was to seek and save that which was lost." No, that is the *purpose* of the Father. But the covenant the Lord made with Abraham was one of great blessing and favor.

It is important to look at the similarity between what God told Adam and the covenant He made with Abraham. The first man and woman were told to *"be fruitful and multiply"* (Genesis 1:28). Plus, they were promised unlimited provision. But sadly, their disobedience caused them to forfeit God's blessing.

It took many generations before the Lord found a person whom He could trust with a new covenant. That man was Abraham. God told him, *"Get thee out of thy country, and from thy kindred, and from thy father's house, unto a land that I will show thee: and I will make of thee a great nation, and I will bless thee, and make thy name great; and thou shalt be a blessing: and I will bless them that bless thee, and curse him that curseth thee: and in thee shall all families of the earth be blessed"* (Genesis 12:1-3).

This is our heritage as saints of the Most High God, to walk in the abundance of heaven. As a born-again believer, you are under the same covenant: *"If ye be Christ's, then are ye Abraham's seed, and heirs according to the promise"* (Galatians 3:29).

***

Claim this covenant without shame or apology because it is God's will to bless His children.

A City of Gold

One day, we will enter into the unspeakable glory of heaven. In John's revelation, he eloquently described this magnificent city – and I believe we need to take the time once more to contemplate what God has prepared for those who love Him:

And I John saw the holy city, new Jerusalem, coming down from God out of heaven, prepared as a bride adorned for her husband. And I heard a great voice out of heaven saying, Behold, the tabernacle of God is with men, and he will dwell with them, and they shall be his people, and God himself shall be with them, and be their God.

And God shall wipe away all tears from their eyes; and there shall be no more death, neither sorrow, nor crying, neither shall there be any more pain: for the former things are passed away.

And he that sat upon the throne said, Behold, I make all things new. And he said unto me, Write: for these words are true and faithful.

And he said unto me, It is done. I am Alpha and Omega, the beginning and the end. I will give unto him that is athirst of the fountain of the water of life freely. He that overcometh shall inherit all things; and I will be his God, and he shall be my son. (Revelation 21:2-7)

As his revelation continued, John wrote:

And he carried me away in the spirit to a great and high mountain, and shewed me that great city, the holy Jerusalem, descending out of heaven from God, having the glory of God: and her light was like unto a stone most precious, even like a jasper stone, clear as crystal. And the building of the wall of it was of jasper: and the city was pure gold, like unto clear glass.

And the foundations of the wall of the city were garnished with all manner of precious stones. The first foundation was jasper; the second, sapphire; the third, a chalcedony; the fourth, an emerald; the fifth, sardonyx; the sixth, sardius; the seventh, chrysolyte; the eighth, beryl; the ninth, a topaz; the tenth, a chrysoprasus; the eleventh, a jacinth; the twelfth, an amethyst.

And the twelve gates were twelve pearls: every several gate was of one pearl: and the street of the city was pure gold, as it were transparent glass.

And I saw no temple therein: for the Lord God Almighty and the Lamb are the temple of it. And the city had no need of the sun, neither of the moon, to shine in it: for the glory of God did lighten it, and the Lamb is the light thereof.

And the nations of them which are saved shall walk in the light of it: and the kings of the earth do bring their glory and honour into it. And the gates of it shall not be shut at all by day: for there shall be no night there. And they shall bring the glory and honour of the nations into it.

And there shall in no wise enter into it any thing that defileth, neither whatsoever worketh abomination, or maketh a lie: but they which are written in the Lamb's book of life. (verses 10-27)

Oh, what a glorious home is waiting for those who have given their hearts to God's Son! But, thank the Lord, we can experience His kingdom on earth. As children of God, we can claim our divine covenant and start living in the awesome atmosphere of heaven.

Chapter Six

Claim Your Royalty

Many nations of the world are led by kings and queens rather than elected officials, and we view with amazement the pomp and circumstance when they ascend to the throne.

Royalty, however is not limited to a handful of blue-blood edindividuals who claim power because of their heritage. As blood-bought, born-again believers, we are also members of a Kingdom family – one which has no rival.

When Jesus died, rose from the tomb, and returned to His Father in heaven, this "Lamb which was slain" returned to His rightful place seated on the right hand of God in the throne room of heaven.

Here is how the apostle John described the scene in his revelation:

> Then I looked, and I heard the voice of many angels around the throne, the living creatures, and the elders; and the number of them was ten thousand times ten thousand, and thousands of thousands, saying with a loud voice: "Worthy is the Lamb who was slain to receive power and riches and wisdom, and strength and honor and glory and blessing!"
>
> And every creature which is in heaven and on the earth and under the earth and such as are in the sea, and all that are in them, I heard saying: "Blessing and honor and

glory and power Be to Him who sits on the throne, and to the Lamb, forever and ever!" (Revelation 5:11-13 NKJV)

"A CHOSEN GENERATION"

When Jesus ascended back to heaven, He retrieved power, riches, wisdom, and all the other blessings described in Scripture. And here's the most exciting part: if it was ascribed to Him, it is also ascribed to us. God's Word proclaims, *"You are a chosen generation, a royal priesthood, a holy nation, His own special people, that you may proclaim the praises of Him who called you out of darkness into His marvelous light"* (1 Peter 2:9 NKJV).

The Greek word used for "proclaim the praises" is *arete* – which means excellence. So when the Bible talks about showing forth the things that are worthy of praise, it lets us know that mankind was made to display this power, this wisdom, this wealth, this honor, and this glory. It's in our DNA!

***

When we understand that God made us to represent wealth personified, we will no longer fight the mentality that He doesn't want us to receive His utmost.

CROWNED WITH DIGNITY

Let me repeat it again: you are God's royalty!

Starting in the Old Covenant, the Almighty declared, *"And ye shall be unto me a kingdom of priests"* (Exodus 19:6).

This applies to you and me as Christ followers. Jesus, who *"loved us, and washed us from our sins in his own blood... hath made us kings and priests unto God and his Father"* (Revelation 1:5-6).

He is *"the King of kings, and Lord of lords... who giveth us richly all things to enjoy"* (1 Timothy 6:15, 17).

***

*We are not only made to represent the heavenly
Kingdom, but we are vital members of it
– crowned with glory and dignity.*

And as a result, it is God's will for His children to have lifestyles that are honorable. This means we are to live in such a dimension that *"we should be to the praise of his glory"* (Ephesians 1:12).

The Lord is depending on us to walk in the manifestations of His divinity so that men and women will worship Him as a result of our example.

BALANCE IS NECESSARY

In Christian circles there is much said concerning the material side of prosperity, and the question is asked, "What does the born-again believer have a right and a privilege to?"

In a society where people are "money" driven, there is plenty of abuse, and in the church, it results in teaching that is often inaccurate. However, in God's Word we find balance. So the question we need to ask is, "Does God want us to have material possessions?"

Let's examine once again the land where the Creator first placed man. It was prime property, abounding with gold and precious stones (Genesis 2:10-12).

It is obvious that Adam did not manufacture diamonds and other treasures. These valuable resources were already in the ground, provided by the generosity of the Almighty. As Scripture tells us, *"All things were made by him; and without him was not any thing made that was made"* (John 1:3).

The mistake many believers make today is that they have given the earth over to the world – to those who are not living in the image of God.

WE HAVE IT BACKWARD!

Even though it was the will of the Father for mankind to have material wealth, He wanted to see these possessions governed by people with a nature that mirrors His. Sadly, we have allowed those who refuse to serve the Lord to possess the majority of earthly treasures, while we as the children of God sit back and act as if we don't have a right to these things of value.

We have it backward!

When God made man, all of the assets of this planet were for his use. Remember, "The earth is the Lord's, and the fulness thereof; the world, and they that dwell therein" (Psalm 24:1).

MATERIAL VS. SPIRITUAL

Since our heavenly Father originally intended that mankind, in the image of God, would be in possession of all these precious assets, He certainly doesn't mind Christians enjoying the things of worth.

Don't forfeit your right to the "good life" by saying, "God doesn't want me to have it." If this were true, He would not have provided these riches on earth to begin with. They were placed here for us to use and to take delight in.

Many have perverted this truth, failing to understand that the material is never greater than the spiritual.

***

It is not the gold that gave Adam his identity; it was the nature of God that defined him.

We aim for the spiritual, not the material. And by doing so we will not be governed by the wrong master. The Bible cautions, *"For the love of money is a root of all kinds of evil"* (1 Timothy 6:10 NKJV). Why this warning? Because we should not love anything more than Almighty God.

When you take hold of this truth, you will not be chasing material possessions, but they will be chasing you – to advance the Kingdom, for a blessed life, and to help you be in a position to bless others.

That is the bottom line of why God so prospered Adam in the beginning. He was to start by developing the Garden, then turn the whole earth into a place of glory, honor, magnificence, and beauty. In order for that to happen, the Lord had to bless and empower him, providing everything necessary for the process to go forward.

WHAT IS THE PURPOSE?

Today, it is still God's intent that we have the best this life has to offer – but not to selfishly hoard it purely for our own benefit. His purpose is for us to take these resources to build the Garden of God wherever we go. This is why we need wealth that only He can provide. In practical, yet biblical, terms, we are to renovate neighborhoods, build homes, start businesses, revive nations, and wipe out poverty.

***

***Whatever it takes, we need to bring the abundant nature
of God into the lives of mankind.***

The words of Jesus are just as relevant today as the moment He spoke them: *"Inasmuch as ye have done it unto one of the least of these my brethren, ye have done it unto me"* (Matthew 25:40).

HEADED FOR THE "GOOD LAND"

God longs to bless us so greatly that we are able to show His glory wherever we go – to take the wealth of heaven and use it to invade the earth. This is how true peace and prosperity will come to our land. I believe our world is tired of seeing man-made economic systems that can crash and burn and leave millions in dire financial straits.

The signs of the times are pointing to a divine economic transfer of wealth from the world to God's people, just as He did when the children of Israel left Egypt with the riches of the land.

Not only did He bring them out of captivity wealthy, but He was taking them to *"a good land, a land of brooks of water, of fountains and springs, that flow out of valleys and hills; a land of wheat and barley, of vines and fig trees and pomegranates, a land of olive oil and honey; a land in which you will eat bread without scarcity, in which you will lack nothing; a land whose stones are iron and out of whose hills you can dig copper. When you have eaten and are full, then you shall bless the Lord your God for the good land which He has given you"* (Deuteronomy 8:7-10 NKJV).

EVERYTHING IS PREARRANGED

As the Bible records, the destination the children of Israel were headed for was much like what God prepared in advance in the Garden of Eden: *"So it shall be, when the Lord your God brings you into the land of which He swore to your fathers, to Abraham, Isaac, and Jacob, to give you large and beautiful cities which you did not build, houses full of all good things, which you did not fill, hewn-out wells which you did not dig, vineyards and olive trees which you did not plant"* (Deuteronomy 6:10-11 NKJV).

The Lord was trying to tell them, "I am bringing you out of bondage and into a land where I have everything prearranged for you to build the life I have ordained."

The Lord had one major request:

> Beware that you do not forget the Lord your God by not keeping His commandments, His judgments, and His statutes which I command you today, lest – when you have eaten and are full, and have built beautiful houses and dwell in them; and when your herds and your flocks multiply, and your silver and your gold are multiplied, and all that you have is multiplied; when your heart is lifted up, and you forget the Lord your God who brought you out of the land of Egypt, from the house of bondage; who led you through that great

and terrible wilderness, in which were fiery serpents and scorpions and thirsty land where there was no water; who brought water for you out of the flinty rock; who fed you in the wilderness with manna, which your fathers did not know, that He might humble you and that He might test you, to do you good in the end – then you say in your heart, "My power and the might of my hand have gained me this wealth. (Deuteronomy 8:11-17 NKJV)

Then God gave them a reminder that is just as real today as it was thousands of years ago: *"But thou shalt remember the Lord thy God: for it is he that giveth thee power to get wealth"* (verse 18).

A MENTALITY OF PROSPERITY

What a glorious plan God has for those who have accepted His Son. He has endowed you with His nature and the resources to build the life He has destined for you, plus enough to share with those who don't yet know the Lord.

***

I pray you are getting excited about the fact that it is God's will for you to live in abundance and to have glory and honor.

We are the kings and queens of God and are meant to walk and live in the finest heaven has to offer. So, we need a mentality of prosperity before we enjoy a bank account of prosperity. This is why the Bible tells us, *"I wish above all things that thou mayest prosper and be in health, even as thy soul prospereth"* (3 John 1:2).

To make this scripture come alive, the concept of abundance must be part of our spiritual nature; we won't pervert or use it for unrighteous living. Instead, we will operate with an understanding that wealth is given to us to promote heavenly, Kingdom living here on earth. This is what God created us to do.

Right now, claim your provision. Declare your God-given right to provision and blessing. Walk with your head held high in the dignity of the King of kings.

Your Royal Heritage

If dignity is in your nature, it's a sure sign that excellence is in your DNA – and that you are committed to the highest and best, and are constantly improving.

You do not possess this quality to brag to the world, but to represent the divine royalty you have been granted.

***

*Some describe humility as "thinking less of ourselves,"
but this is the wrong definition. Humility means
to think of yourself less and others more
– not to think of yourself as less.*

Many who scrape by with few material possessions begin to identify themselves with what little they have. But your identity should never spring from what you possess, but rather from who you are. This is why it is a must to fully understand that you are a child of the Most High God, born of His splendor and majesty. Knowledge of this heritage will cause you to walk in His nature of excellence.

A First-Class Reflection

God implants His excellence in your being so you will use every talent and skill you have been given to the best of your ability for His glory. And you will treat your material possessions the same way.

For example, you might not financially be able to purchase the latest model car, but the vehicle you own should be tuned up, polished, and a first-class reflection of who you are. You may not own a mansion in a gated community, but "excellence" should shout from the way you maintain your property and landscaping.

Every day when you show up for work, you should be quality personified – in how you dress, how you conduct yourself, and in your work ethic and production.

As children of God, we should not be walking around like second-class citizens, barely getting by and doing only a fraction of what we could be contributing to the cause of Christ.

***

Have a serious conversation with yourself and reaffirm,
"Excellence is in my DNA!"

YOUR CROWN OF GLORY

If we show the world who God truly is, by our very actions and behavior people will begin to change, repent, and understand that Christianity is about being the best we can be and having the finest because it is the "God kind" of life.

Yes, you are a royal priesthood, *"And when the chief Shepherd shall appear, ye shall receive a crown of glory that fadeth not away"* (1 Peter 5:4).

If you profess to be a Christian, you have an obligation to represent the royal family into which you have been adopted. You owe it to the Lord to display to those around you what a true son or daughter of the King of kings looks like.

Let me encourage you that your actions from this day forward be in the spirit and the absolute attribute of excellence, because it is part of the dignity God has granted to you.

PART THREE

DOMINION

CHAPTER SEVEN

A RESTORED EARTH

In the first two sections of this book we have examined the Divinity and the Dignity of our spiritual DNA. This brings us to the third important aspect: Dominion.

In our foundation scripture, referring to man, the psalmist writes: *"Thou madest him to have dominion over the works of thy hands; thou hast put all things under his feet"* (Psalm 8:6).

It is not only the *calling* of God for man to have dominion, but it is also part of his original nature. The verse says the Creator *made* him with this authority. This means dominion was grafted into man on purpose – he was designed and built with this authority in mind.

As a result, it was in the very nature of Adam to administrate the land.

WE WERE MADE TO RULE

Man malfunctions when he is living beneath circumstances instead of over them. Why? Because we were made to rule, to order, and to govern. So we are not functioning at full capacity when we feel dominated – whether by situations or by a person without divine authority.

This is why the Bible tells us, *"The Lord shall make thee the head, and not the tail; and thou shalt be above only, and thou shalt not be beneath; if that thou hearken unto the commandments of the Lord thy God, which I command thee this day, to observe and to do them"* (Deuteronomy 28:13).

Man was not created to be subject to anyone but God. So, the Lord commanded Adam to put all things under his feet because he had the DNA of the Almighty.

A UNITED REIGN?

It is significant that when Adam was originally given the mandate to rule and to administrate, both heaven and earth were under the dominion and authority of God. Now the Creator was turning the rule of this world over to the man He had placed in the Garden.

The Father's intention, however, was for Adam to take his responsibility for the jurisdiction of the earth seriously. It was to be a united reign, with each having authority over the separate domains – and they were to work in harmony. Remember, the Bible tells us, "Thy will be done in earth, as it is in heaven" (Matthew 6:10).

***

This was God's plan – the Father ruling heaven and Adam ruling the earth, so there would be a kingdom in both realms.

But after Adam sinned, it caused him to not only lose his soul, but it also resulted in God losing His dominion in the earth through man's disobedience. So when Adam fell, the earth fell with him.

OUT OF CONTROL

In the vacuum of leadership, Lucifer now took charge and began to govern this planet through wicked men. He used the iniquity of Adam to capitalize on the opportunity to establish his own kingdom.

Remember, Lucifer had always wanted to be in control; this is what caused him to be thrown out of heaven in the first place.

***

The devil's goal was to be a supreme ruler, under no one's authority.

When Adam yielded to temptation, Satan pranced around in celebration! His rival was banished from the Garden of Eden, and now the evil one was in total command – with no master over him on earth.

Immediately, Lucifer began to set up his earthly government, complete with rules, orders, belief systems, and moral codes. And before long, the whole earth was out of control. God had lost His domain.

Satan is obsessed with being like God. This is what originally got him kicked out of Heaven. He has always wanted to rule like God. This is his only desire! Satan is not interested in anything else except trying to govern the earth like God rules the heavens. In his own perverted way, he thinks he is a god. Therefore, Satan's struggle with us has nothing to do with religion or religious beliefs. His fight is over power. God gave us what He wants – dominion over the earth.

Let me explain this a little further. Satan used to be a servant of God as an archangel, but it wasn't enough for him to worship the Creator. He wanted to belike God. The Bible declares that the iniquity which was found in his heart was pride. So the Word of God tells how he said to himself, "*I will ascend into heaven, I will exalt my throne above the stars of God; I will also sit on the mount of the congregation on the farthest sides of the north; I will ascend above the heights of the clouds, I will be like the Most High*" (Isaiah 14:13-14 NKJV).

That was his ultimate plan and desire. But God discerned his heart and cast him out of heaven like lightening! Praise God!

Let me pause to explain that often ministers preached sermons about the devil as if he is God's enemy. But the Bible describes *"your adversary the devil, as a roaring lion, walketh about, seeking whom he may devour"* (1 Peter 5:8). He is your adversary, not God's. The Almighty does not have an adversary!

We often think that when this event happened there was a cataclysmic struggle between God and Satan. But the Bible declares that the Creator cast Satan out in the blink of an eye! Hallelujah!

So, when Satan fell, he thought the earth would be his domain to rule. But God came down and scooped up some clay and breathed into the nostrils of that clay and man was born. Then He said to Adam, "Be in My image and have dominion over all the earth."

When Satan heard this, he screamed in anger. Why? Because Lucifer wanted to be like the Creator, but God wouldn't allow it. He wanted to rule like the Almighty, but God would not permit it. So at least he thought that when he fell to earth he would no longer be under God's thumb and would finally have a place to dominate.

But then God made man and told him, "Be like Me." He also told Adam, "Rule like Me." In other words, "You will govern the earth like I rule the heavens."

So now you understand why Satan hates man. It is because you have the image, the authority, and the very earth he craved. To put it simply, we are everything Satan ever desired to be and have all he ever wanted to have. Glory! Glory!

When God made man, He totally ruined all of Satan's dreams.

Now that we have dominion, Satan is under our control on the earth. And just as God had authority over him in heaven, we are to exert control over him here. That's shouting news! We are the devil's new masters and we were created to dominate him. This is the main reason God gave us authority. It was to keep Satan in check and totally rule him and make him subject to us – so there would be peace on earth as it is in heaven.

Friend, Satan knew this. He understood that he could not rebel against Adam anymore than he could against God. He was sentenced to a life of defeat. This is the basic reason Satan tempted Adam to sin against God: to entice him to vacate that enviable position.

With man out of the way, he could regain his rule over the earth once more. And that is exactly what happened. When Adam sinned, it gave Satan a chance to reign on this planet and become the god of this world. So, the battle was being fought over who rules the earth.

When Adam fell into sin, it seemed as if the devil had won, but thankfully, God had another plan.

Things Were about to Change

However, there was a prophecy given – that the seed of the woman would crush the head of the serpent (Genesis 3:15).

This statement foretells the lineage of rulership and dominion that would descend from Adam to Jesus.

Lucifer was able to govern to a certain extent in the earth realm, and God did not express supreme dominion in the earth because He had lost the man He had designated to rule. But when Jesus came, everything changed.

Isaiah gave this amazing prophecy: *"For unto us a child is born, unto us a son is given: and the government shall be upon his shoulder: and his name shall be called Wonderful, Counsellor, The mighty God, The everlasting Father, The Prince of Peace. Of the increase of his government and peace there shall be no end"* (Isaiah 9:6-7).

This tells of God's dominion returning to earth – the government of heaven would be reestablished in the world. And when the Prince of Peace would arrive, there would not only be an *"increase"* of the Almighty's authority, but there would *"be no end"* to it.

This tells us God was not only going to bring His righteous reign back to mankind, but He also would expand and spread His authority until the whole earth was once more beneath the rule of the Great Jehovah.

What a wonderful prophecy!

"THE LAST ADAM"

The promised Messiah *did* descend from heaven, in the form of a Holy Child heralded by angels and born of a virgin.

When Jesus grew to be a Man and stepped on the scene to minister, He declared, *"Repent: for the kingdom of heaven is at hand"* (Matthew 4:17).

He was announcing that the rule and dominion of God had now returned to earth.

***

This was only possible because God had found another Man whom He could rule through – His only begotten Son.

It is why Jesus is called *"the last Adam"* (1 Corinthians 15:45).

The apostle Paul gives us a marvelous comparison of the first and second Adams:

> Therefore, just as through one man sin entered the world, and death through sin, and thus death spread to all men, because all sinned – (For until the law sin was in the world, but sin is not imputed when there is no law. Nevertheless death reigned from Adam to Moses, even over those who had not sinned according to the likeness of the transgression of Adam, who is a type of Him who was to come. But the free gift is not like the offense.
>
> For if by the one man's offense many died, much more the grace of God and the gift by the grace of the one Man, Jesus Christ, abounded to many. And the gift is not like that which came through the one who sinned. For the judgment which came from one offense resulted in condemnation, but the free gift which came from many offenses resulted in justification.

For if by the one man's offense death reigned through the one, much more those who receive abundance of grace and of the gift of righteousness will reign in life through the One, Jesus Christ.) Therefore, as through one man's offense judgment came to all men, resulting in condemnation, even so through one Man's righteous act the free gift came to all men, resulting in justification of life.

For as by one man's disobedience many were made sinners, so also by one Man's obedience many will be made righteous. Moreover the law entered that the offense might abound. But where sin abounded, grace abounded much more, so that as sin reigned in death, even so grace might reign through righteousness to eternal life through Jesus Christ our Lord. (Romans 5:12-21 NKJV)

A Restored Kingdom

Jesus came to reinstate man to the place and position (the state and nature) he fell from. But more important, to restore mankind under the authority of God – so the Almighty could once more have His kingdom in both realms.

God's Son descended to earth with a command from heaven to rule sickness, disease, the wind, the waves, and evil spirits.

***

He brought total dominion back in the earth, and wherever He moved, He ruled.

It was never Jesus' desire to function in this capacity since the world was originally Adam's territory. But because of the first man's transgression, God had to send His Son to *restore* the Kingdom – giving dominion back to man through Jesus.

OUR TIME TO RULE

This ability to take charge was actually transferred from Jesus to you and me when, just before He ascended to heaven, His Divine DNA, which you received at salvation, was being activated in you.

Christ declared: *"All power is given unto me in heaven and in earth. Go ye therefore, and teach all nations, baptizing them in the name of the Father, and of the Son, and of the Holy Ghost: teaching them to observe all things whatsoever I have commanded you: and lo, I am with you always, even unto the end of the world"* (Matthew 28:18-20).

What was the message to be delivered? Jesus said, *"This gospel of the kingdom shall be preached in all the world for a witness unto all nations; and then shall the end come"* (Matthew 24:14).

It was a Kingdom message. Jesus was telling us, "I have returned dominion, authority, and government back to the earth, and you are now authorized to function and rule just as Adam did. You have the same rights."

"IN MY NAME"

Christ was leaving this earth, but He told us to continue to operate in His name. One of the last statements He made before returning to His Father was this: *"In my name shall they cast out devils; they shall speak with new tongues; they shall take up serpents; and if they drink any deadly thing, it shall not hurt them; they shall lay hands on the sick, and they shall recover"* (Mark 16:17-18).

Jesus was commanding us, "Go in My authority, lordship, and dominion. Bring the world back into order, and command everything around you to once more be under the subjection of God."

When Jesus commissioned us to go in His name, He was authorizing us to speak on His behalf. He didn't say, "Speak My name," rather, "Speak *in* My name" – meaning that you declare with the same authority as Christ. You represent Him from a position of power.

However, you must be a member of God's family to use this name: "*Of whom the whole family in heaven and earth is named*" (Ephesians 3:15).

This was the difference between the Apostle Paul and the sons of Sceva, Jewish exorcists who "*took it upon themselves to call the name of the Lord Jesus over those who had evil spirits*" (Acts 19:13 NKJV).

When they spoke the name, the demons didn't respond accordingly. The reason being, even though they spoke the name, they were not in the name. So, the evil spirit said to these impostors, "*Jesus I know, and Paul I know; but who are you?*" (verse 15 NKJV).

This is powerful, because it tells us that demons know those of us who are operating in His name and that we have authority over them. So boldly speak in the name of Jesus!

Paul wrought special miracles by using the authority that was in the name of Jesus. This was possible because, as an apostle, he was authorized and deputized to minister in that authority.

This is a mandate we must not take lightly. But what is our role in making this a reality? Specifically, what is the Lord asking you and me to do?

That is what I will address in the final chapter.

CHAPTER EIGHT

YOUR DOMINION AUTHORITY

Our finite minds have a difficult time believing that God would actually give you and me "command and control" of His work on earth. But it is true.

He not only tells us we have authority in this world, but in heaven itself. Jesus declared, *"I will give unto thee the keys of the kingdom of heaven: and whatsoever thou shalt bind on earth shall be bound in heaven: and whatsoever thou shalt loose on earth shall be loosed in heaven"* (Matthew 16:19).

That's dominion!

Yes, Jesus came to earth to reclaim the Kingdom, but then He handed the keys to the church – including you and me – and said: "Go! Bind! Loose! Order! Decree! Establish! What you declare as lawful is lawful, and what you declare as unlawful is unlawful!"

He repositioned the church and its believers to rule on His behalf, *"and the gates of hell shall not prevail against it"* (Matthew 16:18).

***

> *It is the assignment of the body of Christ*
> *to take the dominion God has given us*
> *and go into the world and bring God's kingdom back.*

The "world" is the Greek word *cosmos*, which isn't limited

to the physical earth, but it includes the systems that have been set up to operate here – the order and arrangement of them on our planet.

RETAKE "THE SYSTEMS"

When the Lord told us to go into *all* the world, this is all-encompassing. It includes:

- The political system, dealing with governing laws.
- The educational system, which teaches not only knowledge, but shapes our values and beliefs.
- Arts and entertainment. We are to invade the music and motion-picture industries.
- The science kingdom, including modern technology.
- The sports system, with its heroes and role models.
- The medical kingdom, with its ability to affect lives.

You may say, "Aren't these just the natural progression of things?"

They certainly are, but since they were set up after the fall of Adam, Lucifer has greatly influenced each of them. This is why the Bible tells us that when Jesus was tempted in the wilderness, Satan took Him *"up into an exceeding high mountain, and sheweth him all the kingdoms of the world, and the glory of them; and saith unto him, All these things will I give thee, if thou wilt fall down and worship me"* (Matthew 4:8-9).

In this scripture we see that the devil had gained access to the earth to establish certain kingdoms, rulerships, systems, and governments.

***

Satan had the audacity to tell Jesus, "If You will just bow to me, I will give You the wealth of these kingdoms."

What was the Lord's response? He boldly replied, *"Away with you, Satan! For it is written, 'You shall worship the Lord your God, and Him only you shall serve'"* (verse 10 NKJV).

GO INTO EVERY SPHERE

Jesus didn't have to worship Satan to have dominion because He knew that in about three and a half years He would be going to the cross and rise from the dead with the divine nature of God. He fully understood that He would once again snatch the keys of authority from the enemy and reestablish God's kingdom in the earth realm.

Today, the assignment is ours: go into all the spheres of our world and bring back order, morality, and rule so *"The kingdoms of this world are become the kingdom of our Lord, and of his Christ"* (Revelation 11:15).

This is the will of God, which has been placed in the DNA of everyone who is born again – to be used of the Father to establish His dominion in the earth.

Let me remind you that *"Of the increase of his government and peace there shall be no end"* (Isaiah 9:7). This means the assignment of the church is to expand and enlarge the Kingdom.

God has promised to help us. He declares, "If my people, which are called by my name, shall humble themselves, and pray, and seek my face, and turn from their wicked ways; then will I hear from heaven, and will forgive their sin, and will heal their land" (2 Chronicles 7:14).

"TAKE IT BY FORCE"

Will we meet resistance? Of course. During the ministry of Jesus, He was challenged and threatened by both religious leaders and government officials, and Scripture records, *"He began to rebuke the cities in which most of His mighty works had been done, because they did not repent"* (Matthew 11:20 NKJV).

As the children of God, we are not here to appease our critics or to take sides; we are here to take over!

The Bible states that *"from the days of John the Baptist until now the kingdom of heaven suffereth violence, and the violent take it by force"* (Matthew 11:12).

We have been made, fashioned, and equipped with dominance on the inside of us to rule on God's behalf. The key to increasing the Kingdom is to find territories in which to rule and conquer.

In the process, never underestimate your adversary: *"For we wrestle not against flesh and blood, but against principalities, against powers, against the rulers of the darkness of this world, against spiritual wickedness in high places"* (Ephesians 6:12).

Our Primary Battle

The enemy doesn't want to yield one inch of territory. We know in advance that he is already defeated, but our warfare involves marching into the systems and orders in which he rules to advance God's perfect plan.

This is our struggle, because *"the whole world lies under the sway of the wicked one"* (1 John 5:19 NKJV).

***

Our task is to reshape culture and society, bringing systems, governments, and rulers into a new way of thinking – with the mind of Christ.

Kingdom mentality and its message must be preached – *"and then shall the end come"* (Matthew 24:14).

As the church, we have been commissioned to take the mandate of dominion into the four corners of the world and proclaim it until we cause a major shift in how institutions and systems operate. As a result, those who have been living under Lucifer's orders and ways will begin to turn and change, to adopt a Kingdom mindset so we can advance the rule of

God in every sphere of influence in the earth.

This is the primary battle of believers because we are fighting against the systems of government, education, media, and science that are often in conflict with the rule and will of God.

Therefore, the Kingdom must be *forcefully* advanced. We are to take ground in the name of Jesus.

WHAT IS YOUR CALLING?

In order to accomplish this, we must understand that there are specific realms or rulership into which God has called each of us.

Personally, I function in the spiritual realm, which means I have been called, gifted, anointed, appointed, authorized, and deputized to be a preacher of the gospel – changing worldly culture into Kingdom culture.

However, not everyone is called to preach. It is not their "office" or gift, not what they were specifically born to do.

Perhaps you were created to be an athlete. If so, your purpose is to go into the sports world to be an influence for the Kingdom.

The same is true if you are gifted for business or to function in the medical field. Your skills and talents are for a divine purpose and must not be ignored or wasted.

If you are a Christian politician, don't be ashamed of your core beliefs. You have been elected to bring spiritual and moral change in government.

***

The obligation of the church is to rise up in our Divine DNA and mobilize the body of Christ to enter every area in which they have been called.

We must use the authority and dominion of God to manifest His rule.

Generational Change

The words of Jesus are still true. You have been given the keys to the Kingdom (Matthew 16:19) – and it starts at home. The generational keys to your family are in your hand. Like King David, there is a person positioned in your bloodline who is going to carry the rule of God and dominion to your children and your children's children.

As I often say, the Lord has anointed someone in your household to straighten every crooked limb in your family tree!

***

It is the will of God to raise up, anoint, and appoint a godly individual with the mandate and authority to affect generational change.

In addition, there are people who are anointed geographically to go into cities, regions, and nations to affect change for the Kingdom of God.

Then there are those who operate in spiritual authority, in a realm of apostolic anointing. When they speak, everything in the heavens begin to shift and move because of this appointment by the Almighty.

I pray you will find your realm of rulership, dominion, and power – and begin to exercise it, bringing everything under subjection.

The Steps of a Good Man

When God says He will put all things under your feet (Psalm 8:6), He includes the world systems we have been discussing. Consequently, everywhere we *step*, we are in control. Nothing moves until we move!

I've heard people say, "Well, if God gave me power, why don't my circumstances change? Why don't blessings come to me?"

Friend, it is not God's will to bring dominion *to* you; dominion is *in* you. This being the case, wherever the Lord calls you to go or whatever God calls you to do, step out in faith. All things will become subject to you.

The Almighty told Joshua, *"Arise, go over this Jordan, thou, and all this people, unto the land which I do give them. . . . Every place that the sole of your foot shall tread upon, that have I given unto you"* (Joshua 1:2-3).

Do not make the mistake of assuming you can step anywhere you please. No, there is divine direction involved. The Bible says, *"The steps of a good man are ordered by the Lord"* (Psalm 37:23).

It is interesting that the Hebrew word for "steps" in this passage means "to incline, or to mount up." This tells us that when God orders us to move, it will always be in the right direction – a step up!

Start Walking

It is the Father's nature to take us from faith to faith, from glory to glory, into realms that are higher than we have ever been before.

This makes me want to shout!

***

Today is your time to step up!

I know this requires faith, courage, strength, and action. In this end-time generation, God is looking for some "high steppers," those who are willing to step up and take the kingdoms of this world. He is searching for those who are ready to ascend into prominent places of law, medicine, or the corporate arena and claim the territory for the Lord.

You are not going to capture any ground by standing still. But since your steps are ordered of the Lord, under His authorization, expect things to change. His dominion is supporting every move you make.

Step into Your Destiny

Now it's your turn. You have been given Divinity, Dignity, and Dominion for a purpose. Pray, "Lord, I accept Your call to go into all the world and bring the message of salvation."

Rejoice! You are about to step into your destiny – it is your Divine DNA!

For Additional Media Resources
or to Schedule the Author for
Speaking Engagements or Special Events,
Contact:

Isaac Pitre
Isaac Pitre Ministries /
Christ Nations Church
600 Sowell Lane
Texarkana, Texas 75501

Phone: 903-831-3959
Internet: www.isaacpitre.org

Order Information

RELIANT
PUBLISHING
A DIVISION OF REDEMPTION PRESS

To order additional copies of this book, please visit
www.redemption-press.com.
Also available on Amazon.com and BarnesandNoble.com
Or by calling toll free 1-844-2REDEEM.

Printed in the USA
CPSIA information can be obtained
at www.ICGtesting.com
LVHW021732130224
771200LV00011B/70